SUM OF MY THOUGHTS

NATEARA U.

CONTENT

NOTE FROM THE AUTHOR

My motivation to write comes from what I see, hear and feel. I share my point of view, in the here and now, where I stand. I want my work received to open hearts and minds, a safe non-judgmental space.

"Keep in mind I'm & artist and I'm sensitive about my shit!"

These pieces are special because they took me through a journey and allowed me to heal. Realizing how far I've come, acknowledging everyone's part in the play and accepting each role. Knowing my responsibility in this thing called life and living it out. Appreciating the situations that made me grow through all of what I went through. Sharing is me making peace with it all, evolving, transitioning and an overall level up. Shedding the weight of the past and welcoming the voyage of the future. Learning to love unconditionally while accepting it can be genuinely returned. Adjusting my view of the picture as it develops, agreeing it's all about *PERSPECTIVE!*

E'Brecia, Jayde, JaMarr II & Catalyah♥ All I do is for the best of you!

Fighting back

Fighting, itself, is barbaric

Just a sheer power struggle

Physical aspects gives the advantage

Takes some learning to roll with the punches

Typically, the strongest survive

Receiving accolades for haymakers

Picture the concept of fighting back

Regaining strength lost in physical fights

By mastering mental strategies to tip the scales

Releasing pain to gain control

Shattering images of fear replaced by courage

Instilling peace in exchange for chaos

Gaining love for self, severing ties with all that creates hate

Fighting back becomes less barbaric and more heroic

More about the need to survive then the need to control

Fighting Fire with Fire to extinguish the flame

Protected

A loose concept of thoughts, ideas and possibilities

Intentions clear, missions set, ready to be fulfilled

Providing protection, security and care, a necessary caveat

We need to know that decisions made include all

Despite the feelings of insecurity within my bubble

Your presence creates a sanctuary of security

Allowing the walls to fall and all guards withdrawn

Access granted, no strings attached, just unconditional love

Creating a space where fear is not welcome

Armor can be hung by the door

All considered, on equal and level playing field

Discrepancies handled within, to satisfaction

Mental sanity guarded from outside influences

Full security package in effect,

We are armed and ready to take over the world!

Waking Up

Slowly regaining conscience as the sun rise fills the space

Waves of emotions flooding my vision and drowning the view

Seeking reconciliation, a clear end, birthing a fresh start

Growth and accomplishments cannot be denied

Repetitive acknowledgement is required

I witness, sense and manifest an abundance of blessings

Appreciating every moment and lesson learned

Accepting the lows adds value to the highs

Beating all odds

Becoming more brave

Creating dreams out of dust

Verifying the path already paved

Waking up to a new day finding a new way

<u>Changes</u>

Evolving through my process

Avoiding traps, schemes and cycles

Trying to clear my head clouded by all these cyphers

Finger snapping lighters flashing incense fills the air

My mind touched the sky

Body and soul ready to fly

Feet grounded and eyes fixed

Ever learning and accepting life

Accepting all of me, becoming more of me

Embracing all that's changing me

<u>Breathe</u>

I need someone who compliments me

One possesses as strengths, my weaknesses

Trust, loyalty and devotion to me through God

Understands growth potential and what it means to sow

The richness of our souls speaks the volumes of what lies within

May he come correct with old-fashioned respect

Satisfy my hunger and thirst, while he positions my mind to rest

When the world tries to convince me you're a tease

You strive for security and always aim to please

Willing to discover my hidden depths without being asked to seek

Never ask for what's not reciprocated

Relax, Relate, Release

When your concern for me supersedes your need

I'll tell myself then, it's okay

And I'll breathe

In Their Eyes

If I hold up my end, they will never see the struggles

The weight and pressure of the world they will never bear

As long as I keep them close, the harm should stray away

I will hold them in prayer and watch them as they play

Making my list and checking it twice

Sacrifices recognized but the burden will not touch their shoulders

Wiping the tears and shielding the cold

Pain buried like treasure when they look in my eyes

They will witness the love and the serenity they all bring

No secrets, no lies, staying away from deception is essential

Yet reality will creep in one day

The world will demand they stand on their own

But for now, security, stability and devotion is what they need

Protect and provide are my keys to succeed

Hold them close, leaving enough room to grow

Speak life as they sleep to awake with more of God's grace

Walk and Talk

Imagine with me...

Encountering intrigue within men

Yet hearts so broken into pieces

Discretion proves to be my most valuable tool

He has the ability to captivate my senses

Acts with reasoning and composure

And possesses plenty common sense, which I see ain't so common

His passion is crazy, he walks and talks with me on his mind

His touch is incomparable, that one crystal amongst the stones

His eyes... that look... discernment authenticated

His intentions, yet to be confirmed, seems well worth the journey

Creativity is who he is, he creates murals with words

Transported to younger years when our souls collide

 Making love magic

His aura provokes thoughts and I don't wanna live without him

Watching for tactical schemes unseen that creates a mirage of refuge

Finding only confirmations and reassurance

Soul ties makes my body yearn for all intricate parts of him

Walk with me through storms and rainbows

Talk to me for ultimate understanding

Seeking Answers

How do you know it's real?

When has enough time passed?

Limits reached of moments in each other's arms

Who can we mirror that has actually gotten it right?

Why is it so hard to find? I hear it appears right before your eyes...

That look that confirms you know right where the heart lies

That touch that can never deny loyalty or being the apple of one's eye

Real life... Lights, Camera, Action

Already to expose and develop

Live in living color, you can lean on me if you will

Not seeking miracles

Just less ordinary and more amazing grace

I crave the lure of stardust and that melanin glow

The vision of my forever place with *MY* person

Looking for the right direction to go

Seems I made a wrong turn back there somewhere

Where do I go from here?

Unbreakable

I stop, take a few to collect my thoughts

My mind is drowning in a sea of retrospections

Your last trip left me slowly circling the drain

Unrecognizable weakness...

I stand, no longer a participant to my pain

I feel guilty I made it out alive, combined with fear of what's next

I hear voices battling on what can be... what ifs

A whirlwind of rebuilding takes place

My mind restored to a place of peace

My heart regains strength

No more emptying without options to be refilled

My body no longer offered as a sacrifice for your short comings

My feelings becomes shatterproof, I bent but never broke

My whole journey is resilient

Not easily moved, future growth a permanent requirement

Indissoluble foundations are built,

The blueprint passed to my descendants

I may bend and sway with the times yet here I stand

I am unbreakable

Transformation

Fire has a way of purifying a situation

Turmoil will make you doubt...

Yourself, your potential, your ability

Still make the change that ultimately upgrades you

Transformation always causes you to get real uncomfortable

By being real with yourself

 Real about the change and real determined

Routes appear outside of what's known

Away from your comfort zone

Transformation is a process, no quick fix

Turning stones to silver and gold

It is all exciting and terrifying

Wonderful and full of anguish

Exhausting and magnificent

A true roller coaster,

But the product is astonishing & miraculous

Take the leap

Reason Season Lifetime

Be conscious of the reason someone walks into your life

Not everyone you encounter has a permeant or special place

Some come to teach and some lessons will come as pain

Your level of awareness will be determine the intensity

Be careful not to get attached with a season

They come and go to keep track of time

Accept the moments of clarity

Appreciate the different perceptions and be clear of intentions

The goal is to learn and absorb as much as available

Take heed to those 2nd thoughts

Mini eye openers both negative and positive

Both attract for different reasons, that's okay

They will teach a lot about them and even more about you

Embrace it

Lifetimes are slow and sneak up on you

No fear or confusion, just a breath of fresh air

Matched crazy, the yeng to your yang in flesh and blood

Lifetime is what all the work is for

Be an inspiration to, as they become your muse

Sacrifice as an even exchange, all of what is given out of returned

Two whole people creating a whole new universe

Entirely for the two of you...

<u>**Selfish**</u>

Many internal struggles

Self-esteem

Self-realizations

Selfishness

They all hold weight

Need constant evaluation

And balance

Looking at you from the inside out

Embracing the place that was destined for you alone

Loving from your overflow to ensure you never run low

All provides ultimate self-preservation

Protecting my safe space

Remove the emotions attached that interfere with self-love

No guilt surrounding self-respect and boundaries

Consistent self-assessment

Always self-seeking, uncovering and being renewed

Building foundations that allow a self-sufficient existence

Being self-centered can be a slippery slope

Plenty self-talk, maintaining the right self-image

Mr. Right

Motivation and inspiration flow freely

Chemistry becomes alive

Natural catalyst make room for human combustion

Stay focused; don't forget reason, season, lifetime...

Watch for signs, read and gauge them clearly

My need to be protected feels irrelevant in your presence

You are guarded yet protective

Selfish and particular with some but indulges me

My fellow antisocial extrovert

Our introduction has taught and confirmed so much about me

You are right

Friendship as a foundation is not insulting

You are right

Encouraging reinforcing the wall around my heart

Being guarded but open to new unconventional

You are right

 My flesh yearns to be fed but satisfied by feeding my soul

Simply right all along

Vacancy's fulfilled unidentified as vacant

My quiet keeper

My stress reliever

Mr. Make me better

My Motivator

Had me sold at that first smile

Mr. Incredible, Senor Amazing

With you I am free to be me, unapologetically

Something I thought impossible, you encourage, me...

Mr. Right on time and I thank you

Confirmation my wants are relevant and realistic

You are real, you are right for me

Perfect in every imperfection

Truly defines lovin' me flaws and all

Participant to the pain

Forgiveness is a road I travel often

Taking the journey for others seems purposeful

Need based to move on...

When the path deviates and I have to forgive me

The rocks are wider and higher

The valley's sink lower than before

Overall the pain of the journey seems in vain

Being a participant to my pain leaves marks, some self-inflicted, mostly with-in

Despite it all the road to travel still exist and has to be traveled

Tread lightly, focus only on the process to heal and grow

Forgiving craves to begin with confessions to self,

On behalf of self, with intent to complete self

Being a participant to my pain leaves marks, some self-inflicted, mostly with-in

My Other Half

Searching for love, while existing patiently til you find it
only now you gotta define it...

What it looks like between the two of you?

What old first can we make new?

The jumps, the leaps and journeys

While making memories, just me and you

That internal glow we all can see...

That spark of electricity when our eyes meet

Starry night gazes with everlasting embraces

Energy of a first kiss

Satisfaction as secrets drip from your lips

Opening doors to places familiar and still unknown

Searching for love that heals past mistakes

The type of love you run to instead of from

It deposits more than it withdrawals

Searching for love without boundaries and restraint,

Unconditional and ain't worried about a damn thing

Flows freely between us, deeper than any ocean

And stretched further than you can see

That outta plain sight but all the way in kind of love

Honorable, respectful, verbal, and inevitable kind of love

Love that demands you flourish from all that was sown into you

Breathing life, promoting growth and that building kinda love

The search for love ultimately leaves you on a quest

Beautiful Tornado

Time will heal all wounds, mending flesh and renovating the mind

Opening your heart and soul to the new atmosphere of love

Realizing there is greatness on the other side of the storm

Neutral ground with endless possibilities of evolution

Admiring and respecting the process of progression

Devoting time intentionally to rebuilding and reacquiring all that was lost

Over standing fragility allows you to be consumed with peace

Tornados destroy yet allows room for mess to be transformed by love

I Gotta Write

Things moving slow but going right...

I gotta write

Mind racing, world slows allowing me to collect my thoughts...

I gotta write

Chasing dreams equals many sleepless nights...

I gotta write

So much I wanna share, but, anxiety breeds doubt...

I gotta write

Never put your pen down, Speak through your storm...

I gotta write

Healing others through my pain

I gotta write

Learning my way through my darkness

I gotta write

The world is in a state of emergency

I gotta write

They don't want you to know melanin is vibranium

I gotta write

Generations to follow need to know the power is already in you

I gotta write

Burning bridges and building more

I gotta write

Learning a new way, views from different horizons

I gotta write

Living life and loving it, never settling for simple existence

I gotta write this out and make it tangible...

Love at 1st Sight

How naive would one have to be to believe?

A look a simple connection of the eyes can create...

So what's Love all about, what's the point, really?

Some say it's merely a feeling, just emotions

Created by a series of "feel good" events

Can change like the wind

When you know, you just know...

Others believe and stand firm on Love is what you make it

It takes time, no short cuts, just work

You get out only what you put in

Depending on what you do for me confirms or denies your love for me

Then there is me, stuck in the grey area trying to make it all make sense

But that one moment, a second

So powerful it changed direction and destination

A wrinkle in time

Ideas once assumed as concrete begin to flow like water

Thoughts and conclusions always black and white blurred to grey,

All 50 shades of them

Droves of butterflies consumed

Magically transport me to dimensions of younger years

Body temperature rising, 50,000 thoughts

I start to stutter when I tried to speak

What is happening, something is taking over and it shows

Impressed by your aura, amazed by the sight of you

God's master piece, and he is the truth...

But how is this happening? Why now?

When your eyes are blinded by pain

Ear drums destroyed by deception

 And touch has betrayed you over again

Sometimes your heart sees

Best day of the year

Birth day is a significant, specific time

It marks a fresh clean start, the beginning of time as we know it

Encountering and at times rediscovering who you are

Sum of experiences from trips around the sun

You have never been some of the places you will go

Never to return to places once comfortable

Forward focus, No time to retake tests

The lessons are clearly learned

A brand-new world to explore, every second a blessing

Smile through the pain and dance in the rain

No do overs, take the shot this time

Say what you mean to say while you have the space

Simply a new day to grow through what you go through

Journey worth taking

I find comfort in knowing the road of life was never intended to be straight and narrow

As you walk, every decision has a twist, we turn, we live...

Imagine never turning to look and seeing a mate to multiply and balance life with

The lessons, the lifesaving smiles and hugs, the adventures that would have never developed

What about that twist and roller coaster transition from higher learning to the cypher of the 9-5

Every action and reaction is what life is all about...

The moments in between the pictures that makes them all worth a thousand words

At the end of the day it's the living of life that happens in the curves, dips, twist, turns and finally reaching the mountain top that makes life all worth living!

Less about the final destination and more about all it takes to complete the journey

Between The Lines

I like pushing buttons...

Not any particular kind, shape or size

No particular rhyme or reason

I just like feel, the way the sensation is received by my brain

Simply entertained...

Nothing over the top, or complicated

No particular type

Just enough to hold my attention and make the push worth my time

Peace & calm goes a long way...

Mutual interactions

Since security is the goal

I crave to be satisfied...

Not that it is hard to satisfy me just gotta mean what you say

And say everything you mean

I am after all, extremely simple with in all my complexities

Many facets so I shine in new and inventive ways

Reflections depend on how the light catches me

Important

Say I'm as important as your little toy,

You know that little hand held device you play with

Work on and send messages through

Now all of this works off a battery, a heart so to speak

You manage it, protect and keep it charged

So whenever you're ready to play, it will be ready and at optimal peak

Many days you're busy, working, playing all the games you want

Messages coming and going

You get a message at 50% that your battery needs attention… Ignored,

Again at 15% this time you see red, clear signs of being depleted

Still opting out of stopping games

decreasing the amount of messages sent or received

5% light dim, things are running slow, some apps not functioning at all

POWERING OFF! SHUTING DOWN ALL OPERATIONS!

Shear panic consumes you

Scrambling to find what you've had at arm reach all along

Seemed to be working fine, the how or how long was none of your concern

Now you wait, allow time to recharge

Hoping today isn't the day you need a replacement…

Branches

Grounded and rooted, there are extensions of me

I breathe for my connections and contributions to the world

Many paths sought out with one goal

Find the one meant to travel through to my destiny

The visible is a mere reflection of what lies beneath

Strong, subtle and sweet with many stories held deep

A tell of perseverance and determination

Every stray branch has a purpose

Each one plays its own part

& stays in its place

Purpose conveyed, accepted and supported

All proceed with one heart one goal, just survive

Bear fruit, plant seeds to survive,

Thrive and create extensions of their own

I accept it

I accept that there are things that you can't comprehend

Or simply choose not too

Love being the root

It's like frolicking with chemistry, with no idea of any elements

How they should relate to each other

How they work together, their reactions with one another

The basic foundations, there's rules to this shit

You need reference points, A starting place

With nothing to build on there's nowhere to go

No balance in the situation makes for brittle interactions

You need more buffers or at least learn the catalyst to combustions

Equilibrium is the goal in all this, gotta be open to level playing fields

Or learn some Musiq and let me teach you

We are dealing with an inability to accept

Or understand what love really is all about

Foolish to have high expectations of it being returned

You can choose to accept it and embrace the change

Or have peace on your journey without me

I accept it as a struggle for you, but I reject it in my life

Clarity in Storms

I often feel overwhelmed and tired

But not the kind that makes you wanna sleep

The kind that makes you wanna run a tub full of water

Just sit there and think

Master plans usually develop best out of desperation

The determination of the rose that grew from the concrete

Ultimate idea of diamond in the ruff

Potential known yet lost at a cross road

Deprivation and sacrifice leads ultimately to comfort and bliss

Knowing your strength is right behind your greatest fear

Jump, trust the process you believe in, it will not let you fall

Giving in to it all, looking towards the hills

From which your help has always come

Go through the storm and ride your rainbow

Bridges

I have never been too fond of bridges

I know they serve a purpose, and are important to some

I accept they allow points that would have never crossed to intersect

I understand the process of getting over them is necessary for most journeys

I appreciate the time cuts allowed simply by their existence

However, the idea of going over and going through

leaving ground that is safe and familiar

To step into something new, the unknown... Is unsettling.

Not knowing what lies on the other side or what's waiting for you

Exciting is relative, your experience, your view

Despite the new opportunities on the other side of fear

Hesitations clouds the path causing stutter steps

I approach a new bridge, riddled with anxiety and what if's

Armed with the confidence

Expectations of successful connections

Breath slowly, let one foot pass the other, until I make it over

Growth cycle

Hitting reset at the vital points is necessary for the journey

The part that allows room for growth and development of dreams

Space to recreate all that is unique

A step back to re-evaluate lack, desires and short comings

It's about finding the path that gives a new approach to an old dream

Hold on to the lessons learned without fear or hesitation

Accept you are a sum of all choices, good and bad

Have no regrets

Embrace all choices, absorb what helps you thrive and bury the rest

It is necessary to start over

Reinvent a new you

Don't you see

It's insane the damage you caused is invisible to you

The irreconcilable differences you created

Mindsets of what is normal and politically correct altered and rearranged

Your choices and decisions ultimately sought out to destroy a whole generation

Conjuring ways to lead me down a path of destruction and shedding

Leaving all familiar and comforting behind, the pain and guilt were too heavy to bear

All dead weight released before attaining the next level

Survivor's remorse weighed heavy on my heart and soul

Determination to protect the packages God delivered

Proved to be more prosperous then protecting you

Looking back only for confirmation of roads traveled and hills climbed

Inspiration pours from the lives I birthed

Confirming the direction change was well worth the pain

Fair Exchange

You don't deal with feeling things appropriately, honestly, not at all

Burn some sage and help these spirits be released

Clear the space about the reality of this situationship

My love for you, I'm accepting and redefining everyday

Fear coupled with a past rooted in insecurities leaves me feeling less

Simply not enough over here and way too much over there

Out of balance and most not in my favor

Reservations halted a friendship that was on the brink of development

I see and hear your muffled emotions and mixed up communication

My interpretation of your subtle reactions don't add up

I deal with my lack and growth in areas

Acknowledge their existence

Accepting yours is just the minimum

Thanks to you I know exactly what I desire actually does exist

I have made peace with my decisions and expectations

Give me all of you in exchange you for me

Or leave me to be, free to exchange love on level ground

From A-Z

Another day of analyzing, bewilderment and crusades...

Believing a new day brings a new way, yet

Confusion turns to contempt without clarity

Denial dragged death into our dreams

Evading the situation as our hearts start to fade

Frustration resorts to crying as conversation

Grabbing and grasping at anything that can pull us together

Hindsight being 20\20 but too late to grow from lessons learned

I wish for no more unfulfilled wishes or promises unkept

Just accountability and consistency

Keeping the transfer of power balanced and in check

Leveling all playing fields, protecting all parts

Making struggle a thing of the past

New day, fresh start, chance to right the wrongs

Opening up to a universe of possibilities with

Passion and Purpose as a light

Queens drippin' melanin and stardust

Reigning supreme to the right of her King

Standing on the wings of forgiveness

Traveling roads undiscovered, making our own way

Understanding the war of the world

Vanquishing all that attempt to divide

Watching, wondering and waiting

    ...for X, Y and Z

Dreams Cry

There is no distinction

Even when I'm awake my dreams cry

They begin to tell the stories they possess

Full of despair and nostalgia

My inner most thoughts come alive and are obvious

I'm no longer able to keep my façade

All secrets shown, it all hit the fan

Me missing your voice, needing your connection

But knowledge outweighs desire

Without inspiration my dream cry

Others unwilling to hear or acknowledge

Silent cries for help with no answer

Open your Mind

Open up and feel the words as you read

Imagine becoming sound

The waves and spectrums you would see

Strong, subtle beats flowing around

Electrifying the air making hairs stand on edge

Envision the merengue or meringue presented as beams of light

Either way a pure delight

Innumerable colors of improv

The whoosh of the air *tornadoing* to finish a pirouette

The smell would have to mirror the ocean

Crisp, clean and smooth

Encompassed by it all, being lulled to sleep

<u>Still Waters</u>

My grandma told me never play in still waters

The water must move and feed into other bodies

Without those connections no life flows

The weight of the water may cause some deep effects

But free water has depth that will forever be unknown

Forever renewed, fluid

Always you

You, my best friend

My initiation to love, ideas of what's right and wrong begin

Limits and boundaries created by your methods of affection

To live and die right there in your arms feels like perfection

Some say I'm crazy but you gotta be there to know it

I lost my vision and gave you the keys

That place was never intended to be your home

My first lessoned learned

You started to masquerade as a confidant

An abundance of creations we share

All the predictions and warnings, not enough to avoid the pain

But... the strength and grounding I found when I let go

I found me, the one I thought lived with you

The one that was the foundation all along

But you...

Impressed by your aura, amazed by the sight of you

Love at first sight, my Mr. Right, my other half

My weakness your strength a puzzle piece

I can freely breathe as me, clear visions right on the horizon

All-Inclusive love, I appreciate *YOU*